To the many conservationists working to save giraffes.
And to my home team—Heather, Hayley, Devon, Willy, Essie,
and Gus. You keep me, like giraffes, standing tall. —SRS

To my friend Nilton —GV

ACKNOWLEDGMENTS

Many thanks to all the wonderful experts at the Giraffe Conservation
Foundation for their invaluable review of *Giraffe Math*, including Julian
Fennessy, PhD, co-director; Stephanie Fennessy, co-director; Michael
Brown, PhD, conservation science fellow with the GCF and Smithsonian
Conservation Biology Institute; Arthur Muneza,
East Africa coordinator; Emma Wells and
Katie Ahl, conservation researchers;
and Claire Gall, administrator.

ABOUT THIS BOOK

The illustrations for this book were created with paper collage, acrylic paint, and color
pencil on watercolor paper. This book was edited by Christy Ottaviano, art directed by
David Caplan, and designed by Prashansa Thapa. The production was supervised by Lillian Sun,
and the production editor was Andy Ball. The text was set in Today SB, and the display type is Brice.

Text copyright © 2023 by Stephen R. Swinburne • Illustrations copyright © 2023 by Geraldo Valério • Jacket illustration copyright © 2023
by Geraldo Valério. Jacket designed by Prashansa Thapa • Jacket copyright © 2023 by Hachette Book Group, Inc. • Hachette Book Group
supports the right to free expression and the value of copyright. The purpose of copyright is to encourage writers and artists to produce
the creative works that enrich our culture. • The scanning, uploading, and distribution of this book without permission is a theft of the
author's intellectual property. If you would like permission to use material from the book (other than for review purposes), please contact
permissions@hbgusa.com. Thank you for your support of the author's rights. • Christy Ottaviano Books • Hachette Book Group • 1290
Avenue of the Americas, New York, NY 10104 • Visit us at LBYR.com • First Edition: August 2023 • Christy Ottaviano Books is an
imprint of Little, Brown and Company. • The Christy Ottaviano Books name and logo are trademarks of Hachette Book
Group, Inc. • The publisher is not responsible for websites (or their content) that are not owned by the publisher. •
Library of Congress Cataloging-in-Publication Data • Names: Swinburne, Stephen R., author. | Valério, Geraldo, 1970–
illustrator. • Title: Giraffe math / by Stephen Swinburne ; illustrated by Geraldo Valério. • Description: First edition |
New York : Christy Ottaviano Books; Little, Brown and Company, 2023. | Audience: Ages 4–8 | Audience: Grades
K–1 | Summary: "Told through the voice of Twiga the giraffe, this picture book shares knowledge about giraffes
through math, using measurements, graphs, fractions, time, elemental geometry, and percentages."—Provided by
publisher. • Identifiers: LCCN 2022017783 | ISBN 9780316346771 (hardback) • Subjects: LCSH: Arithmetic—
Juvenile literature. | Giraffe—Juvenile literature. • Classification: LCC QA141.3 .S94 2023 | DDC 513.2—dc23/
eng/20220512 • LC record available at https://lccn.loc.gov/2022017783 • ISBN: 978-0-316-34677-1 • PRINTED
IN CHINA • APS • 10 9 8 7 6 5 4 3 2 1

GIRAFFE MATH

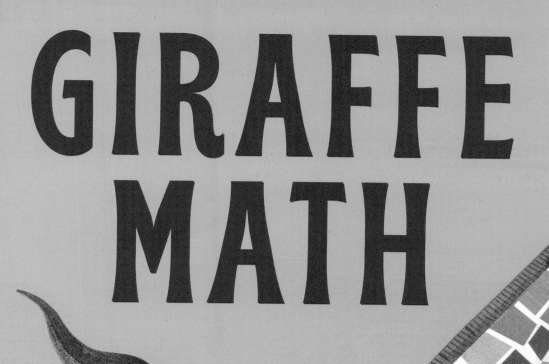

Stephen R. Swinburne

Illustrated by Geraldo Valério

Christy Ottaviano Books

LITTLE, BROWN AND COMPANY

New York Boston

Do you like giraffes? Do you like math? What if you put them together?

Welcome to the world of giraffes and math—we'll look at them from the tip of their ossicones all the way down to their dinner-plate-size hooves. I'll be your tour guide. I know a lot about giraffes. Why? Because I AM A GIRAFFE. My name is Twiga. Get ready for some GIRAFFE MATH!

HEIGHT: How tall are we anyway?

Giraffe numbers are everywhere. Let's begin with our biggest. Adult male giraffes are 16–20 feet tall. Adult females are 13–16 feet tall. We're the tallest animals on earth.

HOW DO WE COMPARE IN HEIGHT TO OTHER CREATURES?

Giraffe:
20 feet

Horse:
6 feet

Third grader:
4 feet

Dog:
2 feet

Isosceles triangle

Equilateral triangle

Can you tell what triangle a giraffe makes when it bends over to drink water?
Sometimes we make an isosceles triangle; sometimes it's an equilateral triangle.
It all depends on how tall we are and how far we need to reach.

We have to be careful when we drink at a water hole, because we must spread
our legs, which leaves us vulnerable to a predator's attack.

Guess my WEIGHT

Male giraffes can weigh up to 4,200 pounds. Female giraffes, like me, average 1,800 pounds. My baby giraffe, Sita, weighed 150 pounds at birth and was 6 feet tall. How much do you weigh? How tall are you?

HOW DO WE COMPARE IN WEIGHT TO OTHER ANIMALS?

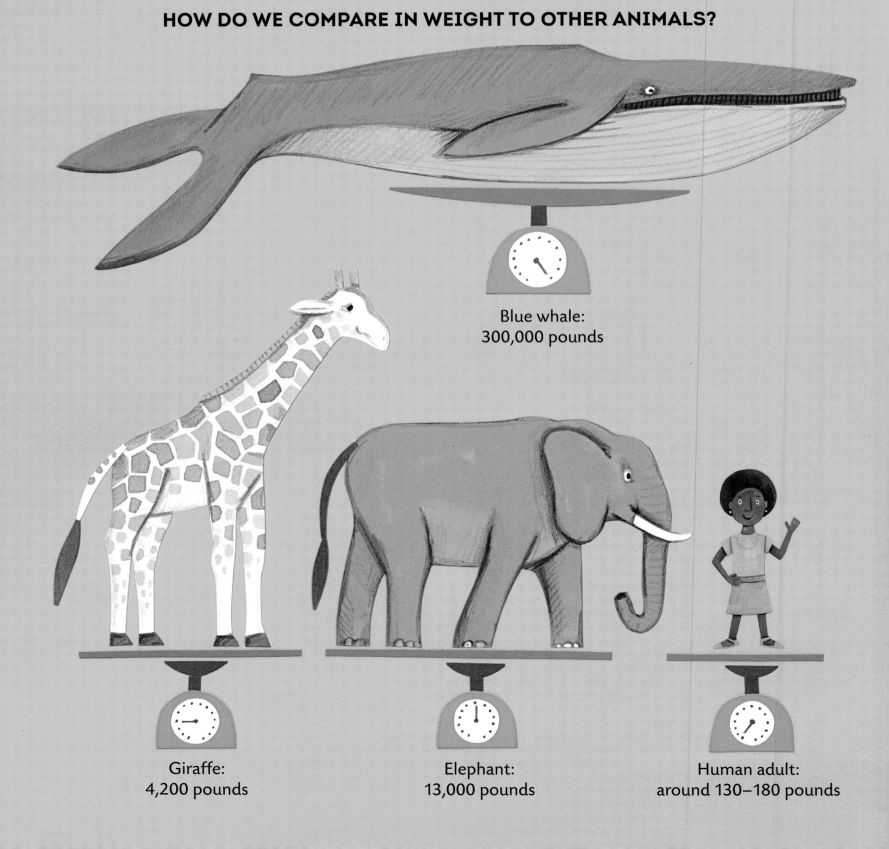

Blue whale:
300,000 pounds

Giraffe:
4,200 pounds

Elephant:
13,000 pounds

Human adult:
around 130–180 pounds

A special name for a group of giraffes standing around is a herd or a tower.

A herd of giraffes walking is called a journey. I love walking with my family and friends.

OSSICONES:
What are those things on top of our heads?

The highest points on a giraffe are hornlike knobs, or bumps, called ossicones. They can reach a length of over 10 inches. If you're seven or eight years old, that is almost the length of your arm.

Both male and female giraffes have at least two ossicones. Some males can have up to five! Males use these horns to fight other males, and that's why their ossicones are sometimes bald. The hair is rubbed off from the friction.

HERE'S THE DIFFERENCE BETWEEN MALE AND FEMALE OSSICONES–

Male:
Long, thick, bald

Female:
Small, thin, hairy

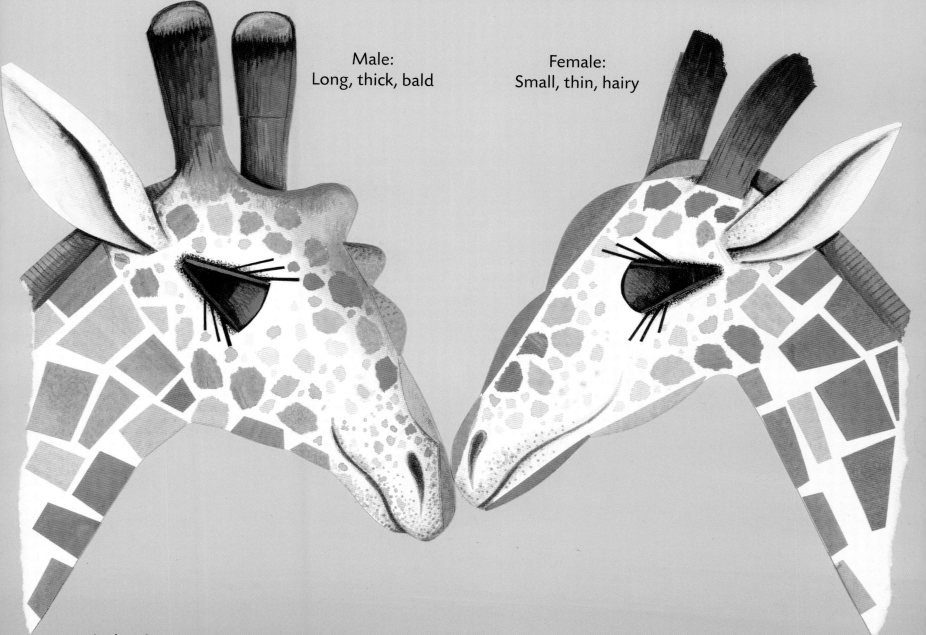

At birth, a giraffe's ossicones are made of soft cartilage and lie flat to avoid injury. They fuse to a giraffe's skull later in life.

Conservationists have attached solar-powered GPS devices to the ossicones of some giraffes to track our movements. They call it Twiga Tracking. They learn how far we travel and where we go. Conservationists keep an eye on us and work to make our habitats safe.

VISION:
I see you!

I bet you've never seen a giraffe with glasses. That's because giraffes have super vision. I might be able to see you from a mile away! Have you ever walked a mile? That's a long distance.

 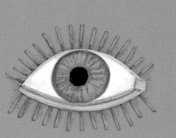 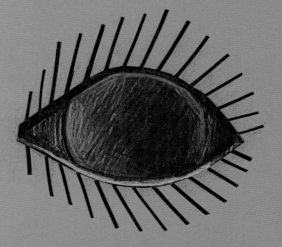

Giraffe eyes are larger than a golf ball. A golf ball is 1.68 inches in diameter. My eyes are 1.96 inches in diameter. Your eyes measure about one inch in diameter, around the same as a quarter.

Giraffe eyelashes are about 1 inch long. They help keep out dust and sand. My eyes are close to the top of my head—I can get a bird's-eye view from this height!

TONGUE talk!

Giraffe tongues are the longest in the world for a land animal. Some reach 1.65 feet, or 20 inches. Your tongue is probably only 4 inches long. And talk about color! Our tongues are black, dark blue, or purple and have lots of a pigment called melanin, which helps protect them from sunburn. Your skin has melanin, too!

Giraffe tongues are covered with thick saliva. That's super helpful when our tongues try to snag some *Vachellia* or *Senegalia* tree leaves that are protected by sharp, long thorns.

My tongue is prehensile. This means my tongue can grasp things by wrapping around them. It's like your hand. My tongue can snatch leaves and pull them into my mouth.

I'm a NECK ahead of you!

Giraffes have seven vertebrae that form our necks. Guess what? So do you! But here's the difference: Each one of my neck vertebrae measures 10 inches long, while yours are about 1½ inches long.

I love my long neck! It allows me to reach high up in my favorite trees to eat leaves and flowers. I feed above all the other browsers, like elephants and kudu. Because my head sits at the top of my very long neck, I can keep an eye on everything going on around me. Giraffes live in herds, so that's many eyes watching out for predators.

What are all those birds around my head and neck? And what are they doing? They're called oxpeckers. I like them because they eat the bothersome parasites (like ticks) on my skin. They're my clean-up crew!

My HEART is superpowered!

Your heart weighs about the same as a baseball or an apple. That's around 5 ounces. My heart is about the same weight as a watermelon, a small dog, or twenty footballs! It weighs approximately 24 pounds.

COMPARE THE SIZE OF MY HEART TO YOURS
AND TO THE HEARTS OF OTHER ANIMALS:

Giraffe:
2 feet long

Third grader:
the size of an apple

Blue whale:
5 feet long, 4 feet wide

Mouse:
the size of a sunflower seed

Giraffes have the biggest hearts of any land mammal. Our hearts can pump almost 16 gallons of blood through our bodies every minute. I need a super-charged heart to pump the blood 7 feet up my neck to my brain.

Swish! Swish!
The tale of the TAIL

My tail is the longest of any land mammal. It is longer than a horse's, a zebra's, or an elephant's. My tail, including the tassel, is almost 7 feet long! Don't you think it makes sense for the tallest mammal on earth to have the longest tail, too? Guess why?

My tail is a first-class fly swatter. I can use it to brush off flies from nearly any part of my body. It's called "tail swishing." The hairs on my tail are ten times thicker than the hairs on your head.

PATTERNS:
Spots and camouflage

Check out your fingerprints. They are unique. No one in the world has your fingerprints. And guess what? No other giraffe has my exact pattern of spots. We all look a bit different. Scientists say my patches, or spots, help me blend in among the African trees and grasses. My spots keep me camouflaged and hidden from predators. But they have another great purpose. My patches are like mini air-conditioners. Each patch acts as a window to release body heat. My spots keep me cool!

Reticulated giraffe

Did you know that there are four species, or kinds, of giraffes in Africa and we each have a unique pattern of spots? There's the Masai giraffe, the Southern giraffe, the Northern giraffe, and the Reticulated giraffe.

CAN YOU SPOT THE DIFFERENCES?

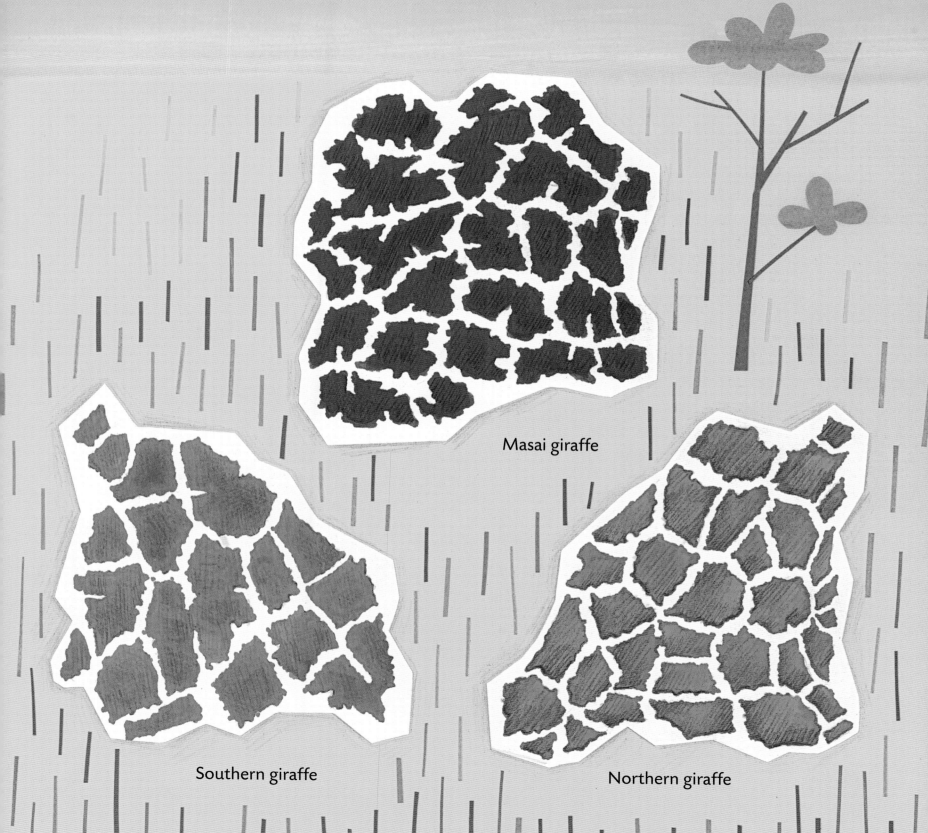

Masai giraffe

Southern giraffe

Northern giraffe

LEGS:
You'd better think twice, lion!

Giraffes have powerful legs, and a lion would not be happy to receive a well-placed kick from a giraffe. My long, strong legs help me fight off predators. If a lion comes near, I lift both my legs quickly and—*pow!*

I'm a good runner at short distances, galloping about 31 miles per hour. Most of the time, though, my family and I move at a slow, ambling walk. Did you know that giraffes walk by swinging both legs on one side of the body forward at nearly the same time, and then both legs on the opposite side?

HOW FAST CAN YOU RUN?

Cheetah: 60 mph

Giraffe: 31 mph

Human: 10 mph

Galápagos tortoise: 0.162 mph

HOOVES and pizza!

Next time you go out for pizza, measure a medium-size pizza pie. Here's a mind-boggling fact: It will be the same size in diameter as my hoof. Giraffe hooves are 12 inches across.

Why do you think we need dinner-plate-size hooves? Hint: Think about our weight and height. Four strong and wide hooves support my weight and my height. My hooves make me feel well-balanced.

Here's something that you and I share: My hooves grow continuously, and so do your fingernails. I wear down my hooves by walking and running across the African savanna. How do you keep your fingernails from growing too long?

Gentle giraffes, gregarious giraffes

Giraffes are social animals, like elephants. When giraffes meet, we rub necks and touch muzzles. We're not big talkers, but you might hear us occasionally snort, bellow, or grunt. Giraffes make great mothers and take very good care of their young. If a mother walks away to feed, another female in the herd will keep watch over her calf. Giraffes are unlike any other animal in Africa. From our majestic height, we oversee the forest in our peaceful and placid way. There's a reason we are called "gentle giants."

The last word from Twiga

I hope you enjoyed learning about giraffes and math. I also hope you know that giraffes are so much more than numbers, percentages, weights, heights, and diameters. We're the tallest and most amazing long-necked mammals on planet Earth. Don't you agree?

MORE ABOUT GIRAFFES!

Giraffe life cycle

Giraffe mothers are pregnant for approximately fifteen months. Females give birth standing up. A newborn giraffe, or calf, falls about 6 feet to the ground. They are able to stand and run within an hour of birth. Calves rely on their mother's milk for about a year, but will eat leaves at four months old. Baby giraffes bleat, snort, and grunt. Adults are mostly silent, although scientists recently discovered that giraffes hum at night. Researchers believe humming could be a way for giraffes to talk to one another in the dark, when vision is limited.

What do giraffes do all day? Giraffes spend most of the day eating and resting. They use their 20-inch tongues and agile lips to strip up to 155 pounds of leaves, flowers, seeds, pods, and bark from trees. And like cows and goats, giraffes are ruminants with multichambered stomachs and gut microbes that allow them to digest plants. In the wild, giraffes can live twenty years or more. Giraffes in zoo captivity live over twenty-five years.

Where do giraffes live in Africa?

This map shows the historical range of giraffes in comparison to their present-day range.

Giraffes have lost 90 percent of their habitat in Africa. In addition to habitat loss, other human threats include poaching by snares. Lions are giraffes' major predator. A sad fact is that, in some areas of Africa, 50 percent of all giraffe calves do not survive their first year. Giraffe calves fall prey to lions, leopards, wild dogs, hyenas, and crocodiles.

In the 1700s, more than a million giraffes roamed across Africa. Today, scientists estimate that only 117,000 giraffes remain in the wild.

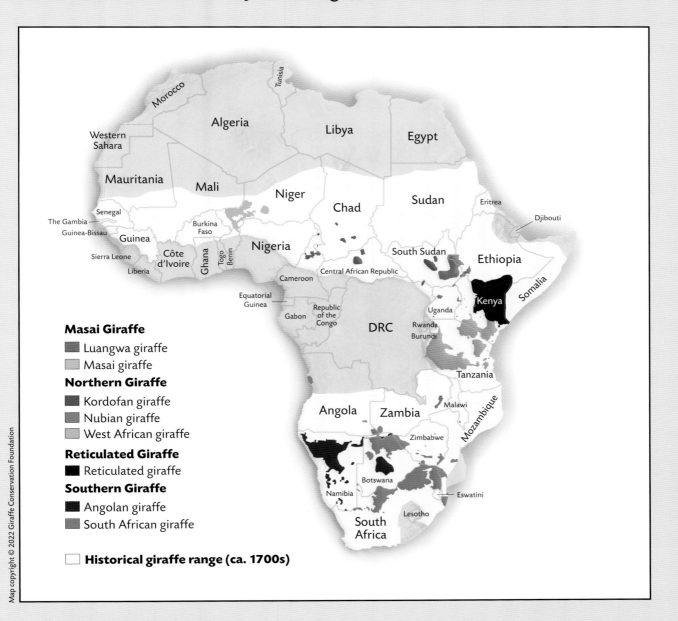

GLOSSARY

browser: an herbivore that eats shoots, leaves, and buds of high-growing, woody plants.

camouflage: the way an animal blends into its environment and helps it hide from predators.

conservationist: a person who helps protect animals and the natural world.

hoof: the covering of keratin that protects the foot in certain animals, such as horses, zebras, and giraffes.

mammal: an animal with hair or fur that feeds milk to its young.

melanin: a natural skin pigment.

ossicones: the knobs, or bumps, made of ossified cartilage on top of a giraffe's head.

ruminant: an even-toed animal, such as a cow, deer, or giraffe, that has more than one stomach. Ruminants swallow their food and then bring it back up again to continue chewing it.

Senegalia: a flowering tree with thorns in Africa. Formerly an *Acacia* tree.

Sita: the number six in Swahili, a language spoken in many East African and Central African countries.

tassel: the dark hair on the tip of a giraffe's tail.

Twiga: the Swahili word for *giraffe*.

Vachellia: a flowering tree with thorns in Africa. Formerly an *Acacia* tree.

vertebrae: the bony segments composing the neck and spinal cord.

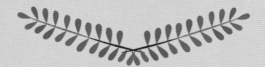

GIRAFFE QUIZ

1. The human heart beats between 60 and 100 times per minute. If a giraffe's heart beats twice as fast as a human's, what is their heart rate?

2. A giraffe's heart pumps 16 gallons of blood per minute. How many quarts are in 16 gallons? (Hint: 1 gallon = 4 quarts) How many cups? (Hint: 1 gallon = 16 cups)

3. Research on wild giraffes indicates they get about 30 minutes of deep sleep a day. How many hours are they not sleeping deeply?

4. How many 4-foot-tall third graders fit inside a 20-foot-tall giraffe?

HOW DID YOU DO ON THE GIRAFFE QUIZ?

Answers to Giraffe Quiz

1. 120–200 beats per minute

2. 16 gallons = 64 quarts and 16 gallons = 256 cups

3. 23½ hours

4. Five 4-foot third graders fit inside a 20-foot-tall giraffe.

METRIC CONVERSIONS

HEIGHT: How tall are we anyway?

16–20 feet (ft.) (4.88–6.10 meters [m])
13–16 ft. (3.96–4.88 m)
6 ft. (1.83 m)
4 ft. (1.22 m)
2 ft. (0.61 m)

Guess my WEIGHT

4,200 pounds (lbs.) (1,905 kilograms [kg])
1,800 lbs. (816 kg)
150 lbs. (68 kg)
300,000 lbs. (136,077 kg)
13,000 lbs. (5,896 kg)
140–185 lbs. (63.5–84 kg)

OSSICONES: What are those things on top of our heads?

10 inches (in.)
(25.4 centimeters [cm])

VISION: I see you!

1 mile (1.61 kilometers [km])
1.68 in. (4.27 cm)
1.96 in. (4.98 cm)
1 in. (2.54 cm)

TONGUE talk!

1.65 ft. or 20 in. (50 cm)
4 in. (10.16 cm)

I'm a NECK ahead of you!

10 in. (25.4 cm)
1 ½ in. (3.81 cm)

My HEART is superpowered!

5 ounces (0.14 kg)
24 lbs. (10.89 kg)
2 ft. (0.61 m)
5 ft. (1.524 m) long,
4 ft. (1.219 m) wide
16 gallons (60 liters)
7 ft. (2.13 meters)

LEGS: You'd better think twice, lion!

31 miles per hour (mph) (49.88 kilometers per hour [kph])
60 mph (96.56 kph)
10 mph (16 kph)
3–4 mph (4.83–6.44 kph)
0.162 mph (0.26 kph)

HOOVES and pizza!

12 in. (30 cm)

Giraffe life cycle

6 ft. (1.83 meters)
20 in. (50 cm)
155 lbs. (70.31 kg)

Further Reading

Giraffes by Laura Marsh. National Geographic Kids, 2016.
A Giraffe Grows Up by Amanda Doering Tourville. Picture Window Books, 2007.

Websites for More Information about Giraffes

The Giraffe Conservation Foundation
https://giraffeconservation.org/
10 Giraffe Facts – National Geographic Kids
https://natgeokids.com/za/discover/animals/general-animals/ten-giraffe-facts/
Giraffe Worlds
https://giraffeworlds.com

Learn How You Can Stick Your Neck Out to Help Save Giraffes

You, your class, or your school can adopt a giraffe. It's easy. Get started here: adopt.giraffeconservation.org